AF477889

The Nowhere Steps

ALSO BY MARK RUDMAN

POETRY

By Contraries: Poems 1970–84

Chapbooks and Limited Editions:

The Ruin Revived   1986
The Mystery in the Garden   1985
In the Neighboring Cell   1982

PROSE

Robert Lowell: An Introduction to the Poetry

TRANSLATION

My Sister—Life (Poems by Boris Pasternak translated in collaboration
    with Bohdan Boychuk)

Memories of Love: Selected Poems of Bohdan Boychuk (in collabora-
    tion with the author)

EDITOR

Literature and the Visual Arts   1990
Other Lives: Biography/Autobiography   1987
Secret Destinations: Writers on Travel   1985

The Nowhere Steps

Mark Rudman

The Sheep Meadow Press
Riverdale-on-Hudson, New York

All inquiries and permission requests should be addressed to: The Sheep Meadow Press, P.O. Box 1345, Riverdale-on-Hudson, New York 10471.

Distributed by Consortium Book Sales & Distribution, Inc.
287 East 6th Street, Suite 365
St. Paul, MN 55101

Typesetting by Keystrokes, Lenox, Massachusetts
The book was composed in Mergenthaler Bembo

Library of Congress Cataloging-in-Publication Data

Rudman, Mark.
The nowhere steps / by Mark Rudman.
p.   cm.
ISBN 0-935296-93-X. — ISBN 0-935296-90-5 (pbk.)
I. Title
PS3568.U329N68   1990
811'.54—dc20   90-30054
                                                 CIP

Printed in the United States of America

for Samuel

ACKNOWLEDGMENTS

The author would like to thank the editors of the following magazines in which some of these poems, sometimes in earlier versions, originally appeared:

Agni Review: "Facts of Life" (sections), "Shelters and Holes"; *Boulevard:* "Casket Closed," "The Unveiling"; *The Denver Quarterly:* "The Bus to the Ruins," (winner *Denver Quarterly Award*) "Courbet," "On Location," "Independence Day," "The Retreat," "The Eclipse"; *Epoch:* "Anything But"; *Grand Street:* "Cliff Seen in a New Light"; *The Indiana Review:* "Turin: Albergo Roma"; *Margin:* "The Nowhere Steps"; *The Missouri Review:* "Conversation: "The Night City"; *The New Republic:* "Aftermath: 1956"; *The New Yorker:* "First Asthma"; *The Paris Review:* "The Shoebox," "The Nowhere Water"; *Pequod:* "Facts of Life"; *Ploughshares:* "Material," "Changes in the Atmosphere," "Trust" "The World Dies And Is Reborn Again Each Second"; *Poetry East:* "Mound Building," "Bottles"; *Present Tense:* "An Eye for An Eye"; *The Quarterly:* "Got," "The Quarter"; *The Southwest Review:* "Winter Solstice: New York/The Caves,"; *The Yale Review:* "My Quarrel with Thoreau."

"Nerves" first appeared in *Poets for Life,* edited by Michael Klein.
"The Shoebox" was reprinted in *The Best American Poetry of 1989,* edited by Donald Hall with David Lehman.
"Cliff Seen in a New Light" was reprinted in *Roth's American Poetry Annual 1989.*

The author wishes to thank The New York Foundation on the Arts for a fellowship during which time some of these poems were written and revised.

CONTENTS

I

“. . . sì che s’io non avessi un ronchion preso,
caduto sarei giù sanz’ esser urto.”

Dante, *Inferno,* XXVI, 44–45

WINTER SOLSTICE: NEW YORK / THE CAVES

The sky's gone underground and tonight
it is the same temperature

as in the cool dripping limestone caves of the Dordogne:
the Grotto de Cognac, stalagmites erect and moist

as if in a constant state of arousal;
Les Combarelles, where scratchings on the wall

could be a constellation, bison, or a wheel . . .
until the guide, with bracelets shaking,

beams her flashlight across the universe's dark interior,
traces an arrow in the hunter's back, as we move,

scuttling and bending, through the openings
from prehistory to personal history—

and though the walls are rife
with animals, it disturbs me that everything

resembles everything else . . .
New York is not a cave, a ruin perhaps, ringed

by several gardens, a city of the mind—
a city of cold rain this day in early winter

growing even colder the deeper I plunge
into the hollow dark, each step forward

over the stones dragging me backwards
toward the Exit that was the Entrance.

The evening lowers, night locks into place.
Without memory, what remains? Without you, what?

"THE WORLD DIES AND IS REBORN AGAIN EACH SECOND"

He was struck by the pure unstinting radiance,
the light blazing so fiercely on the iron railings
he had to shield his eyes,
the sky above the Hudson hard and clear:
the skyline, pink at the edges,
gouged out with a knife.
And the light was everywhere.
It blazed in the window of the barbershop
on upper Broadway just past nine in the morning
the Tuesday after Yom Kippur and Columbus Day,
where the barber was flourishing a straight razor
as he gesticulated and chatted animatedly
with the already well-groomed, salt-and-pepper haired
man in the chair.

It was too early, he felt, for good grooming.
He was surprised that the barber was at work so early,
the straight razor flashing
as he remembered his first walk,
late at night, through the white city,
Merida, in search of a bodega,
when a barber shop was the only shop open on the steamy
street—and he saw the man tilted upside down in the chair,
expressionless, under the glare of the one
dangling bulb, as if he were being grilled
by the police, the barber
drawing the razor across his throat,
wiping the blood-spotted foam onto his smock
with a flick of the wrist,
and, looking in, he was back in front of the painting by Frida Kahlo:
the open scissor between her fingers poised to cut

the artery that binds her to her sister,
their fixed, immobile faces, engraved
with a studied, Aztec attitude toward separation, death.

And now he's harrowed to read in the papers
about the woman, the physical therapist and Buddhist,
who'd left a retreat late at night in Chelsea
and crawled into her van to sleep with the doors unlocked.
And when she woke with her throat slit
roughly by a screwdriver, she still
stumbled up some brownstones steps,
got tired of knocking on the door,
got down the steps, back in the van,
started it up, got as far as a truck parked
all night on the block, got no farther.
She ended with her head on the steering wheel.

Mourning is endless.
One day you walk out and you think nothing's the matter
and then, flash of sunlight on a curb,
you're back in the world of grief, overcome.

CHROME

On the late news I watch hundreds of helmeted riders
almost indecipherable in the dust
tearing up the holes of desert turtles in the Mojave—
and I remember our bravura cycling:
the trick was to go as fast as you could
without being thrown by rock or incline.
Hills leeched of color,
the desert a kind of form,
with rimrock and succulents and gulches
providing borders—boundaries.
Dust and desire.
I wanted to go down toward the desert floor,
where the spines of the saguaro cactus
guarded the sticky pulp I loved,
the sweet, incomparable, centerless center.
O sweet sixteen, to be sprung again and again against
the rock-studded sand, the danger not
in the desert but around it.
The body's oneness with the mind
on the lean machine seemed just right, the body
soaring while hovering close
to the sand as the Honda 125
jounced past yucca and cactus and took
the long dip into the arroyo where the ring
of distant chimney rocks and hills
like space stations receded, and I
twisted the handle-bars like the horns
of a steer to side-wind up and over the rim.
I was thrown only by breaks in the terrain,
grit and stones and dips in the sand,
or by sudden soft patches; or by swerving to avoid
a brush with tumbleweed or a mesquite bush.
Spills were rehearsals for free falling, a way to slow

time down, cease to feel your own weight,
achieve clarity and edge as if edging down
off the concrete onto the sand was the aim. . . .
Circling demoniacally, I didn't notice
the ferocious sun, a fusion of horizon and sky,
or the hawks stunned and motionless as clouds.
Each time, bloody but happy,
I eased back onto the highway,
and set off down the canyon road
into the sun, whitening as it hung
level with the cliff. Once I rode toward it
hearing only the hush of the tires,
the pure elation of it taking my head off as I took
a horseshoe curve at 50 and approached
an even sharper one—the slender cycle shaking apart—;
and I wondered *what to do,* like Porthos
going back to the bomb he'd planted to make sure
he'd lit the fuse . . . when—BOOM!—;
I turned the accelerator handle all the way forward
to slow down—gunning the engine
by accident when the cycle bucked, reared,
and surged ahead—I rose, the cliff's gravel
gleamed, radiant, it was all over;
I could feel my soul leave my body and see my body flung out
over the canyon rim—
it looked as if I'd leap the cliff and fly
into the sun, time gone, space erased,
not a piñon in sight to break my fall, only the cliff
wall, studded with jagged stones.
And I knew if I braked abruptly on the gravel the bike
would catapult me headlong into the open,
so I let go of the throttle—threw up my hands—
and the bike went off the highway, keeled over
and died at the cliff's edge.
I owe my life to letting go.

MATERIAL

When I see the old man again down in the underworld
this morning, him and his son—
how well they get on together, grinning and talking easily

among the bundled packages—
I feel as if I've ripped open some ancient buried
layer of my past; not my own, my blood's.

It's 8:45. They've been there
since daybreak; 14, 16 hours a day,
they're down there, behind the grimed,

grilled windows,
listening to the music of the abacus.
They're a team; their geniality is not feigned.

But in my dream last night there is only
squalor and regression:
My grandfather's underground, toiling in a sweatshop

at Park and 32nd Street,
pistoning between tailors' dummies.
The material runs on and on from the sewing machines,

spills onto the floor, littered with cut paper,
covered with designs for buildings his mother-in-law has drawn. . . .
It all would have happened before I was born.

One image collapses generations, I am drifting
too far back in the genetic code
for a weekday morning,

but it comes to me now as I go down
the subway steps, that maybe it is not
my grandfather cutting cloth

but a more compact, sturdy
version of my step-father—whose father
was a "real" rag-cutter for notions stores. . . .

And so these are not blood ties pulsing through my body
into the ruins of the pewter January light.
Only they are.

At the Chinese laundry
we're all known by our number.
I'm C-17.

CASKET CLOSED

A, the central character
in this tale,
is dead.
His oak casket is closed.

And B is not wrong to say
it's a perfect day
for a funeral,
crisp November air, clear skies.

And C, C is cold,
nobody told her
it would be this cold:
she would have worn gloves.

And D is mad, damned mad
that A would do this
when D would have done
anything to help,

while E wants to know
how it happened,
where, why:
detail by detail.

F's in shock; having known
A for all of her life
she only knew how to look
up at him.

G worked with A
most of his working life.
A was always
"on top of things."

To H he was a great
man and couldn't have gone out
the way he did.
Not the A he knew. . . .

I chimes in it's totally
out of character.
The A she knew
was a pillar.

And J is there to say A
"saved" his marriage
and that he loved him
"like a father."

K—they'd been estranged—
K is weeping,
"the last time I called
he wouldn't come to the phone."

L looks like he's spent
three months getting into shape
for the event
and laying out his clothes.

The mourners are aggrieved.
M is forced to plead
on A's behalf:
it was never anything

personal, had nothing
to do with anyone
present, he didn't want
to talk to anyone

these past few years . . .
why do they all feel

compelled to say
something, M wonders,

and wonders why there are
pines instead of cypresses,
they don't look real,
can't tear his eyes away.

And N, A's widow, is busy
rewriting history,
convincing herself his fall
had to be an accident:

he stood up on the chair
to look out over the terrace
to get a better view
and lost his balance.

Still ruing the means
she tells M that A
always feared he would
die a violent death.

And O, O and O remark
they didn't know that A
had been in such
a bad way.

To P, A's fall was his way
of leaving a scar on the world.
"No. I take that back.
It was an act of courage."

Says Q, the funeral director, to M:
"I can't open your father's grave
unless you pay the back rent
on the family plot."

R asks for his telegram
to be read aloud but it
consists only of reasons
why he couldn't be there.

S, A's best friend, shows up
after the ceremony,
he and A out of synch
of late.

T, S's daughter, offers
that she didn't know A
wasn't her uncle
until she was twelve.

U, A's brother-in-law,
accepts M's salutations:
"I forgive your father.
I know he didn't do it to hurt me."

The events leading up to the end
still puzzle V:
"How come he still gained weight
if he never ate?"

W wails something
about the lost family,
about there being
no one left.

X scoffs M never knew
his father, his mother
poisoned his mind
against him.

Y, too, is right, when she
collars M
after the funeral to stress
A's gentleness.

And Z, A's other oldest friend,
on M's phone mate late that night,
requests that if M is A's son
(and not someone else

of the same name)
would he please call him at . . .
M starts to dial. . . .

NERVES

I'm not really nervous since John warned me about Toxic Shock
    Syndrome,
I'm content with the odds against it.

The jell in these super-absorbent diapers is what brings it on,
he says, and, as is well known, tampons—

I just read the warning again on the box.
If the child saturates this splendidly bulkless diaper in the night

he can loose the jell, which, if it soaks
into his skin, can kill him.

How much are we willing to pay for convenience?
I'm not nervous about catching AIDS from my infected friends,

a simple hug can't bring it on and my friends
are fastidious and considerate.

I've known people who were so afraid of germs,
they brought their own boiled forks and knives

when they came to dinner—whose first words
on entering the door were always—"don't kiss me!"

And as to the spread of Lyme disease, we've been instructed
to walk with pant cuffs tucked into socks;

who would bother, really, when so few cases
have been reported in this state—

but when my son smashes the wiffle ball deep
into the tall wet grass around the house

I hesitate—before letting go and plunging in after it. . . .
When I drive his babysitter home this dark summer noon,

she tells of how she likes the cold, hates the heat,
the insects and scorpions it breeds,

(I've never seen one this far north),
says if hell is always hot then maybe cold is—heaven. . . .

I'm not nervous, merely apprehensive.
It's a kind of voodoo, a way

of controlling fate by inviting the worst
to happen in the form of made-up fears.

My son will still put anything into his mouth,
a fly swatter for instance,

and I play on his fear of bugs to get him to wash his hands
after he uses a public toilet

by saying the germs are like invisible bugs,
nervous that I might stir up phobias.

I'm vigilant where preservatives are concerned,
but lose the battle of Nutrasweet by drinking Diet Coke in his
        presence—

thanks to Alice Miller I can't deny him several swigs—
and I forcibly repress my fears that it might cause cancer in humans.

Then a friend offers that she nearly died last night
from a high fever and she thinks now maybe Nutrasweet brought it on

because she never drinks diet soda.
My father drank at least a gallon of diet soda a day

and he didn't die of cancer: he merely lost his mind.
He feared that nothing natural could kill him.

Now that I think of it, the people I mentioned
turned their cheeks so far to the side I thought

their heads would come off their necks—
the same way my father, in his madness toward the end,

turned his cheek away from my lips
when I went to kiss him.

BOTTLES

> *Misère:* La seule chose qui nous console de nos misères est le
> divertissement, et cependant c'est la plus grande de nos misères,
> car c'est cela qui nous empêche principalement de songer à
> nous, et qui nous fait perdre insensiblement.
>
> Pascal

1

In Bellevue's "Emergency Ward," the diagnosis is not,
as was first thought, "a mild stroke,"
but "acute intoxication" of alcohol and a diabolical
mixture of seven tranquilizers, painkillers, and sleeping pills.
No wonder he couldn't speak . . .
and lay there on the floor beside the bed. . . .
I can't think of anything to say except
"you could have fallen and hit your head."

You might have fallen dead.

(He doesn't know I know the "diagnosis.")

"I don't know what happened to me," he says,
as his eyes scan the bureaus for bottles.
"It's a mystery."

2

I used to hurl the bottles
against the back of motel walls,
away from the hum of the generators
or throw them out of hotel windows,
windows so high above the earth I hardly heard
the crash, only the silent explosion of relief

when I knew the alcohol was gone from the room.
(I never thought of anybody being down below!)
My father never protested, never commented,
never acknowledged the emptiness, the empties,
would simply say, "Be right back,"
and return with the sack
in which the bottles clanged
hollowly like church bells.

"More ice, more ice," he would intone,
in case it should melt before morning.

My son, learning to stand, cocks
his forefinger at the dresser lamp
and utters something like *ite, ite.*

Ice: Gesturing at any clinking glass
he clutches it with both hands,
puts it to his lips and,

sucking and sighing,
tries to down the contents in one gulp,
tossing it back so fast he could choke, or soak,

reaches in, gobbles more ice,
and says *I, I,* through bulging cheeks
as it dissolves; then he coos.

3

I had a high school romance with the bottle too. . . .
And there I am entering the State Liquor Store
in Phoenix on a dark spring night
holding a borrowed I.D.
with the borrowed face
of a 23-year-old,

whose hair stands erect as a rooster's comb,
whose mouth is forced into a joyless grin,
whose eyes glaze over some inner pinwheel;
who looks as buzzed as Yves Tanguy
toward the end...;
frightened, I stand outside,
16 years old, begging a stranger
to get me a bottle.

4

The thrill of it all.
Bottle bottle on the wall.
Ask it anything....

The bottle talks.
Walks not so good.
The bottle knows

your unthought thoughts,
knows better
than you how

you feel about what;
it has plumbed
the unthinkable

alive and risen
filled with air.
Whatever you've repressed

the bottle will tell.
The bottle will tell
you anything unless

you ask,
specializes in spite,
knows by heart one

monologue which ends
with its premise. . . .
"Don't abandon me."

5

Now I want to kneel at a stream and drink,
or drink from a cup . . . or cup my hands. . . .

"I try to rest, my quarrel with myself remains;
I sit, lie down, stand up, never free from thought."

6

One winter, somewhere in the Whiteface Inn
on Whiteface Mountain, no phone, nowhere to run,
where the bottle was delivering a talk
at a Potato Chip Convention, he got me
alone in our complimentary cabin,
lit a fire, fanned it with vodka,
and began the night-long assault
on my mother and her evil stepmother
who'd smile and stab me in the back when my head was turned. . . .
No, the first time was years before, in Miami,
in a restaurant where the red booths were crowned
with bronze and leather horses' heads,
he said the thing about my grandmother being a witch;
afterwards, I was afraid to sleep in the same room with her
though I don't remember believing anything he said. . . .

7

Midnight Lace.

"Hello. Yes this is Mrs. . . . Who is this?
How do you know that? Who are you?
Why, why are you torturing me?"
On the blue-black cobblestones below
her bedroom window she sees

a thin man, dark raincoat, scar
on his cheek, fleeing the corner phone booth.

The bottle wrung his hands
and said, "The husband wants her dead."
Two young women within earshot
swiveled around, outraged.

Bottle: HE HAS THE TAPE RECORDER TELEPHONE HER
          FROM HIS STUDY!

Women: DO YOU MIND?

          You're RUINING it for us!

The bottle nudged me in the ribs,
"This is a real stiff, I'll see you later chum."

And he fled down the aisle as
a soothing male voice murmured:
Don't worry, darling, Scotland Yard
will be right here.

8

The liquid in these bottles was always colorless.
I think I believed it was neutral,
like the stream of hotels and motels
I occupied in his custody.

I always gave him the latest Gillette
for whatever the holiday.
(In those days the razor improved every year:
Edges for every beard.

Mandelstam wrote that though this blade cut
like sedge grass, bent but didn't break in the hand,
it was the product of a dead trust . . .
the shareholders—"packs of American and Swedish wolves. . .").

And once, in Cherry Hill, when he started in
on my mother and her family again
I grabbed his Gillette out of his dopp kit
and held it to his throat.

9

One night, at the end of summer, when the waves
off Montauk were high and running
over that strip of sand,
the bottle followed me through
the dark and fog
where I had stolen away
toward the station to see
my mother's father—
already blind and now dying
in a hospital in the city.
The bottle hated my love for him,
flickered the headlights

of his rented convertible, leaned
across the seat,
"get in, get in," he urged,
his voice like an echo,
slurred, ventriloquial,
as I fled toward the dome's
light glowing down the end
of that narrowing dirt road.
To my left, deafening surf,
to my right, a spiky kingdom:
thicket, heather, dune.

This time he won.
The last train was gone
so he dragged me back,
blessedly quiet.

10

Between my son's *bottle* and my father's *bottles*
I am at odds—
I don't want to drink or eat or dream.

My son is barely one when I take him
to his toddler school, *The Magical Years*.
He fusses when I turn to leave
and so I hold him, and before
I turn to go again, someone's
plucked a bottle out of his diaper bag
and stuffed it into his mouth,
and when he disappears to stand
on the edge of the ring
the older toddlers have been forming,
to stamp a jagged circle,
he moves the bottle to the corner of his mouth,
mumbles *a-go, a-go, a-go,*
and lets it drop.

THE SHOEBOX

I finally broke down and opened the shoebox
which arrived just weeks after my father died.
All winter I had put it out of sight on top

of the bookshelves where I wouldn't be tempted.
The box was not, as I would have expected,
stuffed with photographs, but packets,

wallet-sized, each with a dozen
"snaps," each sequence a kind of story,
and I couldn't have predicted how they would spring out

once I removed the rubber bands
wound tight as bowstrings around the top—
too late now to put them back,

to stop what I had set in motion—
there is no love in them, only
a memorializing will.

A predictable cast, my father's five
older sisters, their several (only three
between them!) issue.

It wasn't that everyone looked demented,
those spinster aunts, those whiz kid cousins,
but that no one looked like they wanted

to be where they were, in that parking lot fronting the beach,
in front of that penny arcade or movie marquee,
clutching that bulging suitcase. . . .

Only one glossy found its way into the box,
the only shot not taken with my father's *Minolta:*
a puppet without strings, no,

a ventriloquist's dummy, all shocked innocence—
me, glassy-eyed, open-mouthed, plenty of space
between my teeth, dangling above

my father, a rotund, baby-faced, leering man,
and his mother, a slack-jawed, toothless old woman,
greedily gazing up at the child as if she were its mother. . . .

The passersby on Times Square look happy
in a miserable sort of way.
In the mid-fifties laissez-faire seems

to extend everywhere except the family.
I plucked the images I didn't like
but when, after a few hours,

I tried to stuff the slender packets back
and close the box, even with half
of the photographs smoking in the wood stove,

they wouldn't smash down, the rubber bands
would not stretch beyond the limit
they had held for a decade,

yet I felt if I was to sleep, to have peace,
the box had to be shut.
The top had to fit snug around the edges.

THE UNVEILING

A perfect day
for an aftermath,
and everyone there
on time,

if unprepared
for the deluge. . . .
This time no one
has anything

to say about A.
Unseasonably cold,
premature November
in the heart.

Nobody mentions the dead man,
he only looks dead
possibly he's ready
to rise.

M is not only a bad son,
he's a bad Jew,
has forgotten whatever he knew
of ritual and convention.

M is also a rotten
husband and father.
The mourners talk
down to him,

they don't mean
to inflict pain,
his father's faults
were legion

but he believed
in the better part
of M. . . . M's son
keeps saying

that he and M
"are the same" (who knows
what he really means)
but A and M

"were the same" too
(who knows what that
really means)
but A never

came up wanting
something to say.
It's a perfect day,
ruined for death

by dying;
too perfect,
like a body in a casket
molded to the earth.

After the aftermath
N's best friend laments
everyone is still
denying, her dead husband

was a carbon copy of A,
the anger, the sulks,
the intelligence
without outlet,

the refusal to reach out—
ever—to others—

the overwhelming
negativity,

blaming the world—
always the world,
poor world!
(At least they spared the earth.)

Nobody understood A!
(Or perhaps they did.)
Nobody understands M!
(Or perhaps they do!)

A and M fit
outside all categories—
yet how can this be
if M's son, before he

was two—pulling down
the wooden tower—
proclaimed
"Daddy and me are the same—"

boys and men.
The sky's
a tarnished mirror
of our communal mood.

*What we see before
our eyes is lost.*
And N left her glasses
behind at the site.

N's concerned
that M's concerned
that he might end up
like A.

They say it's in the genes,
the highs and lows
which lead the body
to the bottle

but M, who has never
in any case known
a middle range,
is fearless,

and feels sure
that this is the one thing
that will never happen
to him

(an odd burst
of absolute conviction
for a man
of so much trepidation . . .).

ANYTHING BUT

No, I want to take it all back and begin over, to,
most of all, change the subject, most of all, to change,
to puzzle the bone of redemption, lightness, grace,
to walk the avenues in the winter light,
to stop and browse, to rummage through piles of old
Classic Comic Books and not remember
the scene in *Oliver Twist* of the bludgeoning
when the blood runs out of her head as I have never
forgotten reading it on the train from
Kankakee to Chicago on my way to the office
of the crack child psychiatrist and electric football fiend who,
smoking his pipe, silent, waited for me to make
a move, to gloat when I won or bawl when I lost. . . ;

I want to change the terms of engagement,
to walk in the winter light without reference to past or future,
light pooling in the gutters, gathering in stillness;
to laugh as I pass the window where strips of white paper form
the bold sign that reads "Divorces: $150,"
or, staring while waiting at the health food restaurant's
        bulletin board stocked with free advice,
to ponder seriously all possible health
remedies for the pain and crotchetiness that afflicts
a different part of my body every day;

I want to stand all afternoon in the Apostrophes bookstore on
        Columbus Avenue
with my friend and, having spotted for the first time
Heidegger's book on *Early Greek Thinking,* read it
as I never would if I owned it and brought it home;
to emerge in the failing light, still
discoursing with my friend on whether the pavement
can serve as the path to thought

since it, too, "stretches far ahead,"
and decide once and for all on the best
translation of Anaximander's fragment,
what it is in nature that brings us to ruin;
if origin carries the seed of destruction;
if time is under compulsion to make us pay for reckless acts;
and if we have still further to fall.

I was telling my friend about my father's death by falling,
of how when I closed my eyes at night I saw him falling,
of how when I walked the streets and looked up at the tall buildings
I would count to the eleventh floor from which he fell
and replay the fall I did not see,
of how the image of falling from a great height has always haunted me,
of how I shook when an Express Mail package came with my baby cup
	and his cameo cuff links,
and had to grab the back of a chair to steady my knees.

II

FACTS OF LIFE

> "Words, as is well known, are the great foes of reality."
> Joseph Conrad

Reversing the Pitch

The afternoon in Miami that you threatened
to tell me the "facts of life" and I,
aged seven, had a vision of these "facts"
as Platonic grids, perfect systems of architecture,
a stone house with an infinite number of rooms.
And I thought your next words would be, "Here is the map—learn
    the routes!"
And the more I begged to know, the more you scoffed;
the louder I heard that huddle of hushed voices,
a secret known to all but me—revealed finally . . .
I couldn't live another hour without the facts!

The prop jet's propellers wind down
over the ocean and the plane seems to hang
in stillness and I go white
and grip the armrests in panic and sputter "d-ad"—
you look up from your papers to peer over
your half-glasses, "What's your problem, doc?"
and I point at the wing and how it looks
like the propeller is no longer turning—
"It's nothing, the pilot's just reversing the pitch."

———

The white bandage of Noxema on your nose
when we sauntered from jetty to jetty
over the shards of broken bottles at the end
of your first year out of work,
and, with slitted eyes and grave expression,
you held forth on the ferocity of bluefish—

how they'd bite the tail off a tuna,
dismantle it, attack and feed:
pound for pound the "toughest fish in the ocean."

And then: "You'd never know it to look at me,
but inside I'm a seething volcano."

More Air

You travelled with one wash-and-wear Polyester shirt.

You wore light raincoats in the coldest weather
and, until the end, always felt "hot."
"More air," you would cry out with a dry throat,
miming the word *hot,* not saying it.
You took the weather personally.

Walking the sub-zero January
streets of Chicago, you were the only
man in sight without a hat.
Your raincoat kept flapping open.
I wanted to cover your head!
____
You accused me of being "literal-minded."
You baited me. You baited everybody!
You hated heat, yet loved the sun:
You wanted to be "burned black."

Custody: At "The Institute"

While I waited into the night for you to finish
dictating your newsletter, *Penetration,*
you set me up at my own Dictaphone:
I invented baseball games
somehow tied by the end of every extra inning;

38

Aparicio and Fox beating out singles for my go-go White Sox,
Jungle Jim Rivera diving headfirst into home
to upset the musclebound Yankees . . .

The psychologists you dragged in after hours
to listen to my game plans agreed
they were "very revealing."
If there wasn't a "David and Goliath complex"
I would invent one!

But by the top of the 17th I'd waited enough,
and, stomping to your door I could see you—
the back of your shirt soaked through,
dictating—"uh, comma, 'because the future
is in their hands,' ellipses, uh, exclamation."

I announced I was leaving.
We could . . . meet somewhere. . . .
You grabbed my forearm. Hard.
"Not   on   my   time."

With bulging eyeballs you mimicked "paranoidal" types,
and rattled imaginary steel balls.
You prognosticated.
"The tests," you claimed, were "foolproof and failproof,"
like a lie detector.

You asked me to take the tests for fun.
"Do you daydream frequently?"
That was my favorite question.
And I know what I answered, but wondered
what I would have done if I were taking the test "for real."

Prodigal with your time when it came to giving free advice,
you mocked my childish reveries over cereal boxes,
and street handouts—the world's freebees—
disgusted by my gullibility.

Your chorus:

"You know what you get for nothing, don't ya?"

Your anger always exceeded the occasion.

An Eye For An Eye

A blizzard. Snowflakes thick as fists.
The Bonanza Airlines turbo-prop comes in low,
bucking the downdrafts, grazing the mountains.
You burst through the synagogue door
with the blizzard howling at your back
and take a seat in the rear
beside a man, a living skeleton,
who shakes and wobbles—every word's a bodily effort.
He has nothing against you,
and you will sing his praises for years.

You only had a few enemies in the room—
my mother, her father, his wife,
their cousins and nephews from Los Angeles. . . ;
and my stepfather, the Rabbi,
who was handing me the Torah.

I could see my grandfather, "Tarzan" Levy,
blind and far into his seventies,
squeeze his white wolf's head cane when the door blew open—
he'd vowed for a decade that if he *saw* "Rudman"
he'd "beat that kike to a pulp. . . ."
(This the same man who baited anti-semites in Europe
before "beating [them] to a pulp". . .)

When the ceremony ended you set out down the aisle,
your raincoat flapping open,
the snow still cold on your hatless head,

40

a quick kiss on the cheek, mumbled praise,
and "see you later chum."

Your loneliness muffled the crowd of well wishers,
strangers with mouths agape and no sound coming out of them.
I wanted to leave with you, I wanted you to leave.
And hurling your shoulder against the door
you plunged back into the storm—
the only man in Salt Lake City
trying to hail a taxi.

Night at the Opera

On your sixtieth birthday you dreamt of entering a theater
and, tired of merely watching the opera,
you wanted to get up onto the stage and sing an aria.
You floated down the aisles filled with dread and desire.
A soldier in black leather was the conductor and the basso profundo;
and when you tried to climb up onto the proscenium,
he grappled you to the ground.
You wrestled. His makeup peeled off like a mask. . . .
It was your father!
"The gentlest man" you'd ever known. . . .

Bolero

But then you wanted to be a composer . . .
until the night of *Bolero*
when, fleeing down the aisle, fleeing "cacophony,"
you waited out the end holding your ears
beside a "white-haired, eminent gentleman . . ."

—your teacher!, a "three B's man,"
who stared at you with astonished eyes. . . .
How could you betray him with Ravel?

Curious, you had to hear it once
but to your relief you hated it, *Bolero,*
anything atonal, the twelve-tone system . . .
Berg, Schoenberg . . .
and you hated to hate it . . .
You "couldn't take the cacophony, the din . . ."

That was it for music. . . .

(When you lost your job you sacked your one
great urban pleasure: tickets to the opera.)

———————

"Everybody does the best they can.
Do you want me to say it again?
Everybody . . ." That was my din, my cacophony.

What made you think you had to phrase things
as though they would be dismissed
without your emphasis?

You'd build me up and tear me down.
(I was never on a level plane for long.)

And so I developed a deadpan expression.
(It sometimes remains stuck to my face.)

I'll stand there expressionless, waiting to explode.
And then I'll explode, and then, some expression returns.

Gunning the Engine

A fishing boat off the Mazatlan coast.
You're running from stern to bow setting up reels
and pointing to where the action is
out in the glittering reaches.
I'm pulling in trash: sea robins, blowfish, barracuda.
Then a school of sailfish arcs broadside—

42

you flick your cigar ashes into the green water—
and, catching the look of delight
that flashes across my face,
command the captain to gun the engine
then mutter, in a voice hot with scorn—
"we're out for marlin."

Matches in the Wind

You never carried matches.

When I bought you lighters you'd show them around:
"Look what Mark gave me! Is   n't   tha   t con   si   derate."
And then it would disappear forever into a drawer.
You'd go out of your way to ask any stranger
for a light, while flicking the dead
ashes of your cigar in their face.
As if proof were needed!

And if this stranger gave you a book of matches
you'd light the whole thing right away, fearlessly,
as the flame flared momentarily around your fingers . . .

then you'd hurl the charred cardboard carelessly away.

Asking for a match could have been
a great way to pick up women
but your choices of strangers were,
as far as I could see, random,

except on our travels when, prowling the beach
you'd go up to some bikinied girl
and dun her, tapping the stub
like a comedian.

Invariably she'd laugh and glance
at me to see if what was happening was real.

But in the city it had to be a windy corner.
I'd huddle against you while you lit match after match
then hurled each little stick into the gutter
sucking wildly on your stub, and maybe—maybe—
you'd get two or three redeeming puffs
before the direful routine began again,
and the next passerby accosted: "Got a match?"

What about a doorway out of the wind?

———

You'd drink more than any man I have ever seen
who couldn't hold his liquor, vodka
in a sixteen ounce tumbler, splash in some Tab
to give it color, then down the vile potion
before we sat down to eat.
Surly, sullen, pawing the placemat
as if to rid it of crumbs,
you'd stare me down with hooded
eyelids and lustreless eyes
as if we'd just entered the ring.
And when I finally nerved myself to say
you spoke with a forked tongue
you had your answer ready—
"I can only speak one way."

———

And this to illustrate you mother's "wisdom"—
briefing the Rabbi, who never knew her, for her eulogy:
you had given her a book of Shakespeare's sonnets in Yiddish;
"I love that book you gave me Cha-lie,
but where could a baseball player get so much wisdom?"
"Bill" Shakespeare, the Yankee outfielder. . . .

Air Conditioner

Sundays we entered your mother's breathless room in Bensonhurst,
and, sweating through your shirt,
tearing off your tie as if it were a noose,

44

guzzling seltzer from a human conveyer belt of nieces and cousins,
you, their hero from "across the river,"
called the nearest Sears:
"I want an air-conditioner for my mother."

"Ma," you whined, "why didn't you tell me. It's a crime."

There was "no one else" to care for her.
Only "Uncle Charlie" could do the job.

They carried her in on a litter like Cleopatra.
The blades of the fan whirred sluggishly.
They set her down.
She reached out her arms—the signal for me to come near.

If she had false teeth, she never wore them,
and it is with guilt and rage that I confess
I hated it when she kissed me:
it left a burning hole on my cheek—

and the more you lavished praise on her the more absurd
the contrast became between what was
and what was *here,* before my eyes:
I couldn't know her through the thicket of your words.

Your mother was your only love.
You never betrayed her.

My mother didn't like playing second fiddle
to your mother; she'd "never seen anything"
like your frenzy for "the old lady."

And when we'd hit the unconditioned air
of the street you'd murmur:
"It's murder out there!"

Do You Daydream Frequently

Old age and madness hit you once and for all
the same midsummer afternoon when your pal,
"a health fetishist and pimp,"
jammed his boat into the dock and you went flying.
After that, everything hurt,
the only solution, such as it was, was sleep,
and you refused sleep. You refused food.
You refused love and turned
your face to the wall when I went to kiss you.

"Hope for the Future"

Psychologists and professors in and out of your employ
seemed dazzled by your polish—
you who were not limited by the mere tunnel of a chosen field,
you, who threw away even a B.A.
to "get out into the *world* of advertising..."

"Expose yourself," was your credo.

You got something for your trouble.

Fast women, fast cars, fast horses.

In the years before I was born
you rode every morning in Central Park,
dashing gay blade in jodphurs.

The women wanted more, your convertibles were slashed, your
     horse died.

You wanted what everyone wants: undivided everything.
Love without effort, mystery without risk.

You treated questions as assaults on your character.

Never one dully to drum up business
(Keynes a convenient hero, "laissez-faire" a solution)
you sweated into the night refining
Penetration at your Dictaphone,
happiest when responding to an "attack"
your clipping service had unearthed

in the *Kansas City Star* or *Delta Democrat*...
"because the 'young turks' are the only
hope we have for the future."

The Facts

When the country was gearing up for war,
you stopped hammering out fresh phrases for *Greymatter*
and got a job selling zippers for Koh-I-Nor...

"To escape the draft,"
your jilted ex-belle from Bensonhurst relates
when she calls me out of the blue
to find you—too late.

Someday you would tell me the story
about the "top secret work" you did for the government:
the two mini-missiles hanging from the wall
were the first installment
of the story I longed to hear.

"You can believe that bullshit if you like.
I'm telling you the facts."

I ask my mother to confirm one version or another.
"What are you, some kind of detective?
Will you stop it with the farshtenkener past?"

And then, unprompted, she claims you not only screwed the maid
but, when a doctor, "a true gentleman," came to dinner,

you called him into the bedroom,
unzipped your fly and "exposed yourself";

my mother knows the story because the doctor
later thought she ought to know "the facts."

Life Raft

That last summer you said you couldn't eat.
Food "won't go down," yet you still gain weight.
When I called you only said you had nothing left to say.
For twenty-five years I received
a newspaper clipping from you almost every day of the week.
When you were in high gear, three or four.

What a thrill, lost in the Midwest,
to get the magnificent torn headline from
the *New York Times,* your rampant yellow pencil
tracing a line to winter . . . through the leaves
I piled till they would go no higher
then dive through; then, fire . . .
"MAZEROWSKI HOMERS IN 10th! PIRATES WIN!"

Then, one day, without warning, they stopped.
I was your life raft . . . yet since the time
my son was conceived you've retreated,
passive, complaining . . . afraid
to take a shower for fear you'd never get dry.

———————

I am not getting used to your not being here.
I still deny. I don't want the truth to leak in.
Who is left to persuade? You're not here.

———————

Oedipus never knew his father;
what could he have had against him?

I never "knew" you either,
(or did I, and does that explain?).

I never knew you, father,
yet I fully understood your code.

Oedipus killed his father because nothing
stood between him and his first intuition.

Dad struck the first blow
at the crossroads.

————

Would you have wept at your own funeral
or had you already done that,
scared of living too long, like your mother?
"I've got longevity in my genes. I'll be around forever."
And yet you spit out that sentence like a curse.

————

Maybe you loved your youth more than I knew—
why else would you have dyed your hair with gunk
like gray-black sooty vaseline
when you were already white at thirty.

Nobody could have lusted more for affection or praise
or been more adept at pushing people away.

I live in the act of your vanishing.

What Does She See

We sat across the living room facing each other
the first night I brought my wife-to-be home
and your first words when we were alone:
"What does she see in you other than me?"
I stared back at you, deadpan my only camouflage.
You misread my glance. "Why are you crying?"
My eyes are dry, but murder is illegal!

"I said," clearing your throat,
"—WHAT   DOES   SHE————"

I mistrusted my hearing, couldn't locate
the motive for your malice.

And yet your rough talk was a kind of preparation
for what was to come in "real life."

————

When you and my mother meet for the first time
after thirty years at the nursery window
you do not speak beyond some formal recognition:
"Are you—Chaaaales?"
"Yes. You must be..."

My Rabbi-father names the baby.
You glower, interrogate the Rabbi.
As he reads, Rabbi-father weeps; blood father winces.
I try to look away.
Your gaze haunts my periphery.

No, not your gaze, your sour refusal
to wear your new teeth....
Later, you collar me in the bedroom
where I am with friends:
"Make sure the Birth Certificate says
the baby's name is Samuel and not Schlemiel."

At the synagogue across the street they're laying beams
across stanchions: a roof is going up!
The sound of hammering rises like trust.
An immense wheel-drum wound with steel cable begins to roll.

————

I can't separate your death from your life,
it had so much to do with falling.

When I try to sleep I see your face as you soar
for an instant before—
You had to stand up on a chair to make it over the terrace.
Not an easy leap for a man of seventy-five.

———

Did you spread your arms over the harbor as you fell
and glimpse boats, tossed on the water like jacks?
Did you think you could fly?
God knows you never showed fear of flying.
But Icarus is a story of a youth.
And the loss of youth is only part of your story.

What's So Funny

You remain my father, for worse and worse,
poorer and poorer, you still mount your horse in Central Park,
still gallop off, serene, unflappable,
into your feckless years;

still arrive drunk at the door to crash
summer parties at the shore wrapped in the flag,
and kill the guests' nervous laughter
with an innocent, "what's so funny?"—

and you are still falling.

———

You "never recovered" from my mother's desertion,
went into "seclusion" for ten years;
but where were you the week she left with me if not in Havana:
whores, alcohol, Cuban cigars,
soaking up rays with the boys.

———

Now you're falling, not like rain or snow,
but as pure spirit plunging
earthwards in soundless space
as the sea winks and glitters
a last time for you in the distance

through the Floridean haze.
The balmy air and palm trees offer no comfort.

Does the heart stop before the body hits the ground?

What Keeps the Coconuts From Falling

I was six when we walked the palmy streets of Miami.
"What keeps the coconuts from falling?"
I saw them tearing themselves loose
from branches, gravity overcoming grace.
How could you remain so calm when faced
with so much possible disaster?

Just before you promised to tell me the facts,
I met a girl in a motel across the road.
We sneaked off into the potted bushes and smoked some Camels.
Then she and her mother escorted me to our room
and the two of you became inseparable for our stay.

It was that week—and they were in our room—
that you started with "the facts."

"Slick Chick"

Fancy vacations every winter to win my love...—
and once, in Hawaii, there was this girl:
close to six feet tall,
black hair down to her waist,
she appeared everywhere with her father.
She towered over him,
a small, bald, flatfooted gnome.
(A *gnomy,* you said.)

Whenever I passed her my body would tense,
my mouth would go dry.

"Whatsamatter, don't you think she's human?"
And you grabbed the girl by the forearm and squeezed it.

"See, see, she's not plastic."
I blanched as she slid her arm out of your grip.

I came back to Salt Lake City "burned black."
A classmate wanted to know where I got the stain.

The Same

And in my dream we are riding a bus together.
Your glances pulverize the other passengers.
But we never speak. You never look at me.
And the bus, moving faster than a subway, but silently,
rolls past a marquee for *Shadow of a Doubt:*
the "two Charlies," an innocent girl and a killer,
lie on separate beds in separate places,
their feet up, their hands folded behind their heads;
she knows he doesn't "tell people things";
she doesn't either, she knows they're "the same"
and that there must be "something wonderful inside him. . . ."

And I reach out to touch your white head
and Sam rises from staring, studious and bemused,
into my eyes, while I slept, our eyelids almost touching,
then drags me, muttering, in his gruff voice
to the mirror, to say—"Look—we are the same!"

———

Walking Times Square the night *Cleopatra* opened.
Did I want to go in? Sure, but how?
You muttered "Press," flashed a sheath of cards
and scooted past the blinking ushers.
"Do you have a seat sir?"
"I prefer to stand."
"Black tie only sir."
"Press."

Barges choked the harbor mouth in the unremitting sun.
Togas and sails listed in the windless air.
"Has there been any spontaneous applause?"

The usher blushed.

You held your nose.
And yanked an imaginary toilet chain twice.
Honk, honk.
"It's a bomb. No action. Let's blow this joint."

And I was still puzzled . . .
why didn't anyone else I had known talk this way?
————————

You had been in business with your sister, what, forty years?
You operated on "your time" while she clocked you in and out,
tallying up your faults,
and your extra hours on your boat when "business was slow . . ."

When she died suddenly her son took over the company,
fired you the next day.
How could he have done this to you, his "Uncle Charlie,"
self-confessed "retired bankrupt"?
————————

"This is the sort of thing that happens to other people."
Looking around the Psychiatric Ward, I agreed.

"Your hair was white when you were a child.
There was no evil in you then."

Whatever I said was "right," and thereby nullified;
you'd thank me for my "time" and sink back into your chair.
————————

This pattern persisted a mere—dozen years:

You had "urgent things" to tell me, I had to see you "right now . . ."
I'd linger, hovering, while you bantered,
drummed up errands, or masked yourself with whiskey

and geared up for an assault on the usual cast of miscreants . . .
drawling my name like a mantra . . . *"Maaaarrrkk"* . . .
waiting to deliver your final goad
until my body landed on the other side of the threshold:
"too bad we never got a chance to talk."

What did I think you could convey: the facts?
What "facts" could you reveal to me at twenty?
Not the facts of life any more surely,
but something about yourself, or about you and me,

father and son.

(One fact remained: ruin.)

My Last Weekend of Waiting

You found X's presence loathsome
since he went on the wagon,
but you would meet with him every summer evening
to watch the sun go down.

You each squawked "it's dog eat dog,"
to the prevailing winds, to the walls,
and added the salt of "Darwin" to the stew.
"It's not so," I risked. "People make choices."

You boomed in unison.
X, the buffer, played the heavy:
"Get outta here, Childe Harold.
You're in the wrong century."

Thanksgiving in the Suburbs with Mighty Joe Young

"It's a waste," you announced, baring your gums
to reveal the periodontist's stitches
crisscrossing like a waterline.

"I've outlived my usefulness."
The other old geezers, hands folded on laps,
stared at the wall-sized television screen:

two drunken bullies getting the gorilla drunk in the cage.
Someone sighed, hung his head and muttered: "They shouldn't
      do that."
And you came to life—"but that's the way it is;

the lust to control the unknown,
the abuse of nature.... Look at us!
We're wasting space!"
              ———
You weep throughout the kitsch play
I Never Sang for My Father.
But then you start to talk about it in a demented way,
obsessively, yet cooly, making each shake
of your head ponderous and slow,
"how true it is for so many, how sad,"
but not of course for *us*—

The play becomes your vindication.
It is I who haven't loved you enough!
(And this too is true.—)

S.O.S.

The last time I saw you alive,
in the Ward, where the ping pong balls idled
under the torched plastic windows,

after you again lamented that *I*
"never had a childhood" and,
as if the two were one, how painful
it was for you to watch me
with my "psychosomatic asthma
gasping and wheezing"
down a basketball court—
I risked another question:
had you ever "seen anyone?"
Your voice eerily level, you shrugged.
"Never had need of it."

Remember our ping pong games?

You put spin on the ball.

And you asked for do-overs.

But you repeatedly confessed, unasked,
to a "Pygmalion Complex"
and married my mother to mold her
and to wrest her away
from her bullying, abrasive father,
who spanked her with newspapers when she came home
after dark from life-drawing class.

"The Unbelievable"

Your voice was breaking and I could hear
the ocean echoing on the line in Miami. . . .
"It's like being . . . in exile . . . I hear so . . .
little . . . good news . . . these days. . . ."
And then you wept.

rescue lingo—this one time and one time only—
to your heart's content.

And this was your one S.O.S. whose "manifest content"
let others lend a helping hand
without a diagnosis.

III

"We must reject that prejudice which makes 'inner realities' out of love, hate, or anger, leaving them accessible to one single witness: the person who feels them. Anger, shame, hate, and love are not psychic facts hidden at the bottom of another's consciousness: they are types of behavior or styles of conduct which are visible from the outside. They exist *on* this face or *in* those gestures, not hidden behind them."

Maurice Merleau-Ponty

that once faced the sea out of necessity,
have all been sold.

Ten years.
You lost your father, then I lost mine.
Now the ozone's wearing thin
and it never gets cold enough
for you to put your sweater on.

The black-red water never reaches the drain.

INDEPENDENCE DAY

1

Something in the radiance of swallows' nests,
in precise meaningless shapes and movements,
like a rabbit's nostrils twitching in isolation

or the sudden metamorphosis of straw into light;
or stories into thresholds; something
in the nature of celebration,

in shadows under trees,
in the many names for late afternoon,
in the night that has only one name,

in the flags released from attics,
in the megaphones sprung from silences,
in floats bursting out of torpor,

in the release that comes with the loss of unity,
in the wind even if the wind is the last
free thing.

In the dark, after the fireworks have dimmed,
another story grows to trouble our sleep;
a night creature topples

the garbage can, digs, licks
bones clean, rips
diapers, peers into eggshells, milk

cartons, spews coffee grounds,
and finds, after all that work,
nothing to eat, nothing to sustain life—

GOT

1

In the clear even light of early fall,
let loose entering the courtyard
of the Sculpture Garden, my son takes off,
shouts to Picasso's goat,
crawls under her, tries
to climb over, to ride her, slithers
off even as I hold him on, goes
after her swollen bronze teats
startled that she will sit still
before the guard booms "Go...";
his ecstasy knows no bounds
like that of a man finding a woman he has long
desired, spread out
on a bed, waiting, quiescent.

2

His obsession began last summer
when goats took over his waking
and sleeping mind and he woke
every dawn with the word "gO,"
like got with a soft *t,*
on his tongue, the intonation rising
only on the second syllable,
the gutteral a mere
springboard to the glorious vowel, ascending,
the noun a spur to the verb;
and as we poured through *The Book of the Goat,*
he gave the same democratic "gO"
to the Nubian ("most popular") as
to the Toggenberg ("aristocratic")

to the unnamed goat who made it
with forty-seven nannies in less than
an hour when they lost count.

3

The grass is sparse on the sandy soil
in her backyard, where, tethered
to a stunted pine by a long rope
the goat is all fur and bones,
its slitted retinas mimicking
its thinness. Curious,
yet still disinterested,
the goat didn't jump back when Samuel
gyrated around it, approaching
and avoiding, reaching out
to touch and then
recoiling,
the chemistry between them so intense
they could have been proclaimed
Boy and Goat right there,
though it's possible desire
never has an object
but, seeking points of rest,
circumnavigates circles.

It was his babysitter's goat.
One morning she pulled up
with her husband waiting in the truck
asking could she take him back to her place . . .
What could we say? We'd only
known her for three days, said
go ahead, spent
the rest of the morning
discussing our discussion.

ON LOCATION

1

Did the camera know when it followed her to the cliff's edge
what would happen? That she would

leap? The director never tells the actors what will happen
in advance. The cliff rises sheer above the gray-black

waters. Night advances as a filter covers the lens.
"Let's do it again, and this time, don't look

like you know what you're going to do."
She walks briskly out to the cliff, like someone

who wanted to shake memories out of her body,
sits crosslegged where the grass is matted down.

Medium shot of cabin interior. She sits before the fireplace,
in profile, alone, then rises and stares into the fire.

A man comes up behind her and puts his arms around her shoulders.
She lowers her head. And walks out of the frame.

2

Rustling, a rotting log tossed over a small stream:
it wobbles as she crosses and enters

a dilapidated boathouse, tilting seaward. . . .
Jumps up and down. The boathouse shakes.

A slight smile on her face. She glances out
a chewed hole in the boarded window toward a spot

on the rocks where a woman hands a child a banana,
which he squinches in his fist and grins.

The tide has come in. She starts to roll up her jeans, stops.
Her expression seems to resist hesitation . . .—"It's only water."

She knows it's high tide now and that as long as
she hugs the shore she'll be safe.

"Eat it, don't mash it." The child holds out
his fist, grins, and squeezes.

———

"It drags. It's too meditative."

"It needs a violent death."

———

3

A woman spreadeagled on the lawn.
The child wedges himself inside the *v* of her legs.

The child plucks the tops of wild roses from the road's edge.
The petals stick to his palm. He carries them home on the run.

The child eats roses like the raspberries he picks
deftly out of the knee-high bushes.

He does not hear the sound of bees in the flowers.
A woman's voice on the soundtrack: "Don't."

The child empties a watering can over his own feet
and regards them as if they were a distant country.

And then he's gone again, around the barn, the bend,
down to the road, where the only traffic is

AFTERMATH: 1956

In later years I woke so often
in that monster's twisted position
I thought he was the key—
his fear of women and his longing
for them as he hovered at the edge
of the lake covered with radioactive fog
where they bathed...;
that monster with a monster's appetite
and a man's precise, fastidious desire,
howling, as a stranger now, for a woman
he loved before fallout
from the bomb put barky fur on his body
and added horns to his head.
The monster wanted to die if he could not love.

It has taken me this long
to realize that what kept me awake nights
for years after the movie of the end
was something—my life—which had preceded it.
The waste landscape on the screen
wasn't so different from the landscape I entered that night:
great gaping groves of elms,
the milky scurf of space stretching nowhere,
the prairie heaving on all sides,
the broken seated theater running
The Day the World Ended—
shot in a dingy low budget black and white—
on the darkened shut down Main Street
in Chicago Heights.

FIRST ASTHMA

I must have been no more than six
or seven that autumn afternoon

because we left that town
by the time I was eight.

Two taxidermists. Twins.
The house was cut back from the road.

The forking dirt paths strewn
with bits of straw and wire led to the sheds

where the taxidermists divvied up their spoils—
a refrigerator shed and a shed

where the wooden bolt was not locked.
The padlock on the one shed door

I came back to and back to
hung like an anchor on a chain.

———

Not a blade of grass on their land.
The walls of the sunken living room crawled

with the black sad beaks of the ducks
craning their necks on twining hooks and platforms,

the indelible black-green of their feathers,
the same black-green as the dull flannel

the songless indifferent hum of the landscape,
the ferocious dry rattling of the cornstalks,

the crows whose shadows pooled on the ground
after their bodies had risen, the sun, which

never again appeared that day, the eyes
that were the only sign of a soul I could see . . .

I tried to hear where the hum was coming from
and, kneeling between the anonymous stalks,

I thought my ear was cusped at the source of sound,
the joy a slow and steady rising,

a lightness in the wind's song I knew could last
for as long as I stayed

out of doors, where things were not bereft, and fixed
beyond imagining.

————

Torn open animals stunned on shelves.
Litter of screens, bottles of dye.

Inside, Hap's wife Maggie
asks what I want to play.

I say, "Gin Rummy."
My mother looked so lovely

as, balanced on the porch rail,
she shifted in her shawl.

————

I remember everything about the day
except not breathing, except

the story of my tense heaving chest,
I, who have apprenticed myself to origins.

As Billy and I circled the stagnant pond,
not a bird flew, not a leaf fell.
Billy glided. I lurched, I flailed.

"Look," he said, pointing to the
ripple in the pond's still, tan water.
"That's a water moccasin. The pond is full of them."

Suddenly I felt very heavy, as if
Billy were leading me to my death and I
was defenseless, I could not find my voice to say

"let's go home," or simply leave alone,
I couldn't see the snakes but I could feel
them near, their cold wet skin, hissing and coiling.

Billy led me down into the basement of the Model Home,
and said not to worry even though the snakes
could crawl through the mud and reach us where we stood.

It would be our hideout; no one would find us here,
we'd put up a tent, move in supplies . . .—
and while I contemplated this secret retreat

Billy disappeared up the stairs
and closed the door. It was locked.
There was no way out. But I would wait.

Billy'd be back any minute. . . . It grew dark.
My skin tingled as before an electrical storm.
And I could feel the snakes coming near,

slithering their last few feet through the wet mud.
Panicked, I put my fist through the glass
and squeezed through, the jagged shards

slicing my arms and hands.

5

Mud-caked and bloody, I went straight to Billy's house.
His mother said I'd find him "down in the basement,"
where I found him, in his rumpled white socks

staring into the window of the washing machine.
His tan mocassins whirled in a confluence of suds.
"I got out," I offered. Billy stared fixedly ahead.

His Dad had come in, calling "Billy," and as I walked out
I could see the pile of small shoeboxes parked by the door.
Why was everything there new and shiny and clean?

Billy never apologized; he forgot, or erased—
He seemed surprised, the next afternoon
that I was reluctant to come out and play.

6

But the afternoon my stepfather gave in
and brought the Daisy air rifle home
I had to run out right away, my pulse

racing, to show the gun to Billy.
His mother called him up from the basement.
"Wow!" Billy was impressed!

He admired the gun, asked
politely if he could "twy" it out,
leapfrogged his front steps,

brought it down with all his strength
and cracked it in two—precisely at the joint.
Billy handed me the two parts.

The heat trapped in the heartlands singes the skin.
It was cool in the shelter's entrance

and we thought it would be good to have a girl.
Why not Inge, nicknamed "Pocahontas,"
that quick, lithe, dark-eyed beauty?

3

After an afternoon around the shelter
digging foxholes against an infantry attack,
when Karl went for a dip in his pool,

Pocahontas and I retired to my backyard,
stripped off our suits and aimed
the spray hose at each other,

pressing our thumbs into the nozzle
to widen the arc of the rainbow...
It was then that her father arrived.

We toweled off with our bathing suits, giggling.
His glowering aggravated the heat
and after that he put his bulk in their doorway

and crossed his arms when he sensed me near.
How could she be the issue of that surly Swede,
blocking the doorway with his bulk,

brooding like a walking thundercloud...?
Now I had to sneak around the back of her house
and hide in the hedges and throw stones at her window.

She'd lean her elbows on the windowsill and smile.
And once she led me to a secret marsh
where a breeze blew mist through the cattails

and the quail rustled.
The marsh made slurping noises.
There were bubbles everywhere.

Someday, she said, when she had
her own canoe, we'd paddle out
past the lilies to the mound together.

I became an addict of late afternoon
light and shade and only looked at nature
when I was on my way to see her.

There I saw the wilderness breaking up—
parceled fields. But as I walked
the thick, sprawling, porchy suburban streets,

the bushy, brushy, elms and oaks and maples
still leaned down onto the pavement as I got lost
in the knots of their loopy shadows.

Let be, I thought, I'd rather have had
an hour under the hose with Pocahontas
than swim forever in that stupid pool.

4

I had a pup tent in our basement
where I hoarded supplies. I'd wad up
a piece of Wonder Bread and make it last

until I fell asleep. I loved the musty
dankness, I loved the beams holding up
the ceiling, I loved the string

hanging from the light socket, I loved the wall
of pure imagining
and the patient rider on the other side

of the wall, who, after tethering
his horse to the backyard faucet
leaned forward in the saddle—

but I don't think Pocahontas
ever entered our house, much less
my tent, and I don't think, after

the fall, when we moved into an older
house in an older
section of town, I ever saw her again.

5

The shelter was never anything more
than a hope, and a hole—stopped by rockface—
hammered into the recalcitrant earth.

It was the pool that brought dire thoughts:
the slatted fence that rose to the level of the diving board,
the round basin, which when emptied,

looked like a meteor had gouged it out,
the unnatural deep "blue" of its cement bottom.
It was a pool for drowning, too small

around to swim in—except in circles.
And toward the end of our first and last
June in that house, I was pulling back the sky's

white glaze curtain when a patch caught fire,
and shook, as if fanned by a sudden wind.
I stiffened in contemplation of the end.

LOVE IN THE WEST, 1965

I stepped out on Sunset Strip alone
in the pitiless even hewn light
like a detective with no case,
and found my way to Hamburger Heaven
to meet my mini-skirted cousin
for a star-filled lunch.

Her mother had worked on *Death Valley Days*
which came on after the news.
Her father had been an agent.
My cousin was a crash course in cool—
a year younger than I was,
already out of high school, her face

was mobile, expressive,
a quick study in innocence
(not stemming from any lack
of experience)—and nerve.
Mascara made her look more pure.
Sitting across from her I remembered

the leaves bunched on the pool's
scummed surface as I walked up the steps
to her glassed-in desolate house
set against a stark cliff
in Hollywood Hills,
where I'd watched her watch her father—

splayed skeleton in royal blue pajamas—
struggle to sit up in bed
in the last stages of leukemia.
After lunch, a traffic jam

disrupted our top-down speed
toward Santa Monica

and she let go of the hot red wheel,
stood up and frugged to the beat
of "Satisfaction." Then, in one
seamless motion, eased back down
and floored it when she saw
an opening in the line of cars.

THE QUARTER

In a meterless taxi she brings it up.
I can't talk about it. Not now.
The driver overcharges.
Why did I trust
this stranger, this moonlighter?
When the reluctant quarter he pours
into my palm slips under
the seat I demand another.
The driver curses: "What's a quarter?"
I pull the seat off and crouch
among the gray wadding.
Nothing shines there like a coin.
And the three-quarter moon rises over a park
brilliant and lucid and cruel,
the side of its face hacked away.
Vengeance? Whose?

And if I start
to think about
the child's death now
when will it end?
It's dangerous:
going down steps
everyone is suddenly motionless—
a murmuring frieze
on the ascending escalator.
I don't know what to call it,
a place in the mind,
a hole, a tear, a gap,
the mind can only go around.
A fuzz around annihilation.
Waking and sleeping,
it impinges, ungraspable grief.

And in my dream the plane,
wobbling upward for a quarter mile after takeoff,
noses down into the warm ocean,
carrying loved ones,
and those not loved well enough.
Waking, the river stiffens with ice.
The rivers stiffen.
The fog splits off in jagged rifts.
Tugboats pass like hearses through the sluices.
And the joy, like levitation,
I feel near my son turns
to lead, then pushes like a steel bolt
through my bones, pins me down.
What do we have to know of hell
that heaven cannot teach us?
The quarter's gone.

IV

"The flagstones were still visible, and Frank walked as if he were
sure of every inch of it. The poplars closed in, then parted, and
they were on the cliff, and Tom could see its edge, defined by
light colored stones or pebbles.

'The sea's out there,' said Frank, gesturing. He hung back from
the edge."

Patricia Highsmith

TURIN: ALBERGO ROMA

for Mary Morris

In the Albergo Roma, I spent one night
in the room where Pavese died.
Another night in Turin and I might have died too.
Something about the milky cast to the sky and the wet
November weather and the slow wind easing in from the Alps.
The night Pavese took his life,
the light would not go on in his room.

He killed himself at the end of August.
The skin darkening on the body keeps the darker gods at bay.
It seemed I was the only man not there on business.
To keep down the panic rising in my chest
I chatted up a stewardess over grappa,
told her about Pavese's doomed love affair
with the blond American actress.
The stewardess did not care.

I set out for Santa Stefano Belbo,
but squandered the afternoon wandering
through the galleries and down the railroad tracks,
which never converged, to the outskirts,
where I saw a mechanic lying dead drunk in an oil slick,
and two hooded urchins riding a bicycle in tandem,
dragging a can on a string, and heard
the lonely malevolent sound of that rattling.

Did Pavese take his life in Turin
to keep it on the map?
In this room where the light still does not go on,
death is a kind of heat, of company.
Was it the light in his room Pavese missed?

Was it light from the stars?
Was it the light of God
untouched by his mania for solitude?
It wasn't light from the moon, cold and remote.
And I can tell you, the next room is no different.

THE RETURN TO ABILENE

There was a railroad in Abilene.
I used to listen to the boxcars coupling all night,
And on the nights when I would lie awake
The moon shone on the fields below my room.
Barns and haystacks glowed.
No city I have seen compares to Abilene.
The vast flat distances on all sides are endless.
They stretch to nowhere anyone would ever go.
Children play unattended in these far fields
Not far from where my father built his fallout shelter
And my friends and I spent one winter stockpiling cans
And counting days and nights—until the year 2000.
Abilene isn't the center of America.
It's the center of the world, arctic and tropic.
And when I lived there all I could think about was leaving,
And once I left, I was distracted, wracked
With the desire to go back.
There's now a toy where you can reconstruct Abilene
Out of plastic bricks and posts and dirt roads.
But which Abilene, and when?
The new saloons have everything over the old ones.
Whiskey you can drink without hangovers,
Computer quail and outlaws you can shoot and shoot again
        and no one dies.
When I was gone, nothing reminded me of Abilene.
With the rugged look rampant over America's cities,
The Abilenians wear pointed boots and tapered suits,
Like the Milanese.
I don't know what happened to Abilene.
Does it matter what I shall do for a living there now,
After so many years away?
At my birth the mother-gods said Go West,
The father-gods said Go East.

East and West are equidistant from Abilene,
And my first sentence was rumored to have been
I want to get out of the barn.
I walked. I was happy. I never wanted to leave. I left.
Because in spite of the changes back to nature
And the resurrection of the railroads,
Even when the moon is not quite full, say three quarters,
It looks so cold and lonely in the vast empty black
Throwing light on landscapes you can never see by day:
On immense distances, and faraway places, and memories
I came back to forget.

THE BUS TO THE RUINS

But it is on the way to the ruins that I see
what will await me, to go is to follow,
over the dry dusty road,
past the fields where celica grows, to submit
to the lurch of the bus and when
it stops look beyond the broken fence,
to where the worker wears a box from a six-pack over his head,
some hundred schoolchildren pile on,
the aisle fills and the black oven
in a backyard smokes,
and—in the Merida outskirts—
white bulls overrun a cement block
housing project in a dried-up marsh,
and a back fence gathers
the blue and green and aquamarine of the gulf,
where frigates soar beyond shadows
and palm trees and rose-colored stones,
and a child molds his "sad castle" only to tear it down . . .
and the bus breaks down beside a black tin
and burlap shack with a sign chalked in—
"Tiendo 'San Francisco' " and a pot-bellied man
savors a Coke at a roadside stand,
the rock guitarist on his rose-colored tee shirt
exploding into notes,
and behind me a man in a white suit dabs his forehead
and confesses to his seat mate,
"I'm a lonely man, doctor,
I get headaches to remind myself I'm alive. . . ."
Police vans crowd the roadside,
two men face each other down in a grove,
(which one though is the "perpetrator"?)
and uniformed men are coming in

with enough guns and ammunition for a small war,
and I know the ruins stand at the day's end,
without doors, without exits.
And if we praise ruins why not the ruined man.

THE NOWHERE STEPS: Uxmal, Sayil, Chichen-Itza

1

I walk through the ruins holding my son's hand
which he wrenches away, runs, falls
on the jagged stones at the base of the pyramid
gashing his forehead. The red blood's
garish as it runs through his blond hair—
as if the gods here could still draw blood.
Or is it the dead. They all know how to hurt.
(At this the dead are expert.)

The Mayan sun needs human hearts before it can move on.
The blood red glow won't run on its own power.

2

I walk through the ruins holding my son's hand.
Wrenching himself free he runs.
On his tongue walls are "gorges," ruins "rooms."
"More rooms," he orders, as he bolts
from stele to stele.

He thinks the jaguar and Chac Mol are there for him to mount.
He treats the eagle as if it would fly when he climbs on.
He has the right idea.

He can clamber up a pyramid step by step in seconds flat
and never get down.
He can fix his gaze on Quetzacoatl
and after several seconds of deep silence
put that plumed serpent in his place with one word: "fwoggy"!

He can detain the owner of the motorcycle in the parking lot
while he rakes the gears and brakes
and turns the mirror upside down to face the roadway
and, when he sights an armadillo on the road's edge,
recognizes what it "really is" under its shell . . . "daquicweeno!"

A god and a worm are equal in his eyes:
he would rather follow the worm.

He runs through the great playing fields
where the victors lost their heads,
his legs moving rapidly as a centipede's—
doing the hundred with a record number of footsteps.

3

The ancients got the better of time, they are still
driving an obsidian knife through nose bone.
The man receives it stoically. The woman is still
pulling a rope through her tongue.

My son trips. The ruins catch the look
in each visitor's eye as if to say:
Look both ways then plunge ahead: Forget.
Love me for what you see is missing.

4

We move off known paths through thickets.
I hold on tight to his hand.
Vines spring around me like a trap,
thorns pierce my flesh, I hold on tight
to his hand and whisper keep very still.
In a jungle clearing in Sayil
he stares the eyes out of a granite phallus
alone in its own thatched paradise.

5

There's not a ruin that can't be
brought down, or a country
in ruins that can't be raised;
not an obscure hillside, dust and bones,

a dog, and children hawking nuts,
that can't attend a miracle.
The ruins are all that's left. Praise the ruins.
Praise Chac the rain-god's snout.

And when you get tired of praying for rain,
and sacrifices pall, before
you start to eat your own heart out,
find something else, in praying for, to praise.

Rise, ruins, and bless the living
who walk among your broken forms,
who pull up beside you in the same
sea-green Volkswagon,

who walk in the heat as the sun beats on their heads,
beats on the loosed stones,
and they think *should never have come,*
added waste to waste . . .

They're all you have, these vatic hustlers,
uninvited, uninitiated,
yet willing to walk your unmarked paths and stray
through the thorns:

Don't banish them from your dried-up springs
and cenotes.
They have come to be changed,
to be arraigned.

It is here, among your fierce, austere shapes,
your relic relentless gaze,
that these travelers
let a little water out of the soul.

It is these travelers who,
walking over the dead of ancient cities,
feel a little more mortal
with each checkered step.

6

In the same place, traveling, the child and I
inhabit different worlds.
"Ba ba black sheep" 's the only song in the world today,
the gods and calendars pretexts
for a glimpse of a mut mut, that black and gold
flash in the branches,
even a woodpecker taking aim.

7

Standing stockstill on top of the pyramid,
I think about my father's fall from grace
then his fall, literally, from a high place.

We walk through ruins where men with hoe and machete
still clear paths for the gods
who never appear,
walk up steps that lead nowhere
and catapult this turret into space . . .

THE NOWHERE WATER

We ate alone in the immense dining room.
She got me to eat each night
by saying any meat was buffalo meat.
The desert had the silence of one who waits.
Cool water, clear water—she sang.
Her voice soothed my deepest blood
as I listened to her sing it over and over;
she knew just how to prolong

cool—clear—water—.
The desert was vast and empty.
Water nowhere, neither cool nor clear.
My one friend lived in a trailer in a dust bowl.
I'd wander off alone and once
got far enough away to where
the bleaching neon of the strip
dwindled to tinsel.

Everywhere we went men were after her.
One clear night we were walking home
hand in hand in the dark.
No moon, but the road was lit
by gas station globes
and not-too-distant hotels,
when a silver-haired man
behind the red wheel of

a white Caddy convertible
stalked alongside
and offered us a ride.
She gripped my hand; panic
coursed through us, our spines rigid.
"Don't look, just keep walking."

Soon she would be married again.
What a waste of beauty—and all on my account.

There is no love like the love
of sons for mothers.
And the seedy silver-haired man,
and his measured, robotic voice,
has hunted me since—
and enters me tonight
through The Talking Heads' searing,
apocalyptic version of the song. . . .

These were the best moments of my life,
alone in Vegas for six weeks
keeping a beautiful woman company
while she obtained her divorce.

DODGE 'EM

You're alive, and there's a certain vibration.

In the rankness of this underworld,
that felt like a stable if it didn't smell
like a stable, the cars, dangling
on poles attached to a turreted dome
like the giant heads of a hydra,
lurched forward in a feverish spasm
when the operator threw the switch,
picking up speed abruptly,
then, if you took a breath and took your foot
off the pedal, stopped without warning;
I mean, it didn't *get up* and *go,*
it hesitated for a moment, like a golf cart, in a kind
of stunned silence, and then, *c-chung, c-chung,*
off it went, 0–5 miles an hour in no
seconds flat, a cinch, until
kids with tickets in their hands, kids who seemed
to know each other, who may have lived,
like my friend in the trailer park, in Las
Vegas all year around, clamoring, clambering,
descended on the gate, converging on line like a flock
of sparrows coming down on the same place
at the same time from everywhere,
unaccompanied, as far as I could see, by their
mothers—and I felt at that time I didn't want
my mother to watch and wave: the love in her eyes
embarrassed me, I was all she had
in the world, all she would ever have,
and I'd corralled a dodge 'em,
I, five years old and an Easterner, a greenhorn, an absurd
figure in a starched white snap-button western shirt,
string tie, shiny cowboy boots, and Stetson

which engulfed my eyebrows:
I'd just wanted to drive the car,
I'd just wanted to drive my car around the circle,
not run the other boys into oblivion,
and as they smashed into me at the turn
I spun around against the traffic,
nicked and bumped each the time they passed,
a dozen rowdy boys, all several years
older than I since we lied at the gate
about my age, my mother and I;
we were conspirators then, my mother
and I—I didn't panic till my hat
flew off and went under the rubber
bumpers and tires, only then
did I begin to wish it would all
end. It was
the longest ride. My tears were banked.
And I knew my face was distorted,
and I knew I would have
destroyed the ride if I could have—
it wasn't that they'd bent my hat
but that they went after it
and smelled it as a shark smells blood.
And when the spinning stopped,
and I got out, and gathered up the hat,
my mother, standing at the guard rail,
her eyes dim with love, took my hand,
and spoke: "Do you want to do it again, dear?"
But at least she didn't go on about the hat.

You're alive, and there's a certain vibration.

THE RETREAT

> "What attracts me is elsewhere, but I don't know
> where that elsewhere is."
>
> E. M. Cioran

The Hudson looked like a sheet of tin as we drove north
and my son, who wants to be where he's going, piped up:
"I want to go to my country. Are we there yet?"

The quiet of night is not haunted in La Anna.
No one's on the street.
There isn't any street.

I recognize the eerie stillness,
the moon contrapuntally racing through the clouds.
And I know the cold dampness of this night will grow dreams

of violent urban conflict,
gas masks, ambushes, broken glass.
When I leave the city my dreams encircle it like a track.

I remember these roads I have never driven,
the stream's intrepid murmuring,
the roof tin that intensifies the sound of rain,

the infra-red vests and hats my neighbors wear
as they pace their backyard fences
even though hunting season is long passed,

the shed stocked with toys and racks of coiled hoses,
the yard littered with rusted stovepipes.
The trees bend even though there is no wind.

A stone-studded hill rises to a level
where a railroad track might have been,
and two deep ruts filled with turbid water run parallel.

The hills are in upheaval and the earth
looks like the outside of the inside
of this fever, yet gapes, with a wonderful awful rawness.

The house is set behind Frey's white-framed
Funeral Parlor that juts out of the woods
like a newly capped tooth.

My neighbor's silhouetted behind white drapes.
This is the "real" America but it's easy
to get mixed up, the reality and the dream.

On the road to Stroudsburg, in the light of day,
they're scattered everywhere—funeral parlors,
and boarded-up honeymoon cottages, and shoestores.

The drivers lurch over the white line.
They drive with their lights on in the middle of the day.
I don't know why there's such obeisance toward the dead here,

or why the living claim so little for themselves,
or why, when my wife and son disappear
on the deserted Main Street to get him a pair

of high tops, no one in the empty shoestores where I go
has seen them, yet when they reappear his feet are clad
in sun-yellow high tops with lavender soles.

On days like this, traveling in America,
I think a thousand miles put only distance
between town and town.

THE ECLIPSE

I was looking out the window, at nothing, and listening to the wind hurl rain and branches against the screens. And I began to sense the full presence of a world one does not see.

I was looking out the window screen, not at nothing, because the small pines had put out new fuzzy branches in the week-long drip, and because things had no shadows I saw them for what they were.

I was looking out the window screen in the morning silence and I remembered walking to the car and the sound of a cello pouring through a window screen—at nine in the morning—in an unremarkable parking space between two houses. I stood a long time with the car door half open and my foot on the door ledge and didn't want to leave.

I was looking out the window screen at the fog and damp. I still can't see where the birdsong's coming from. When I look out there's only a decapitated mouse twitching on the driveway, and a trio of sparrows pecking at the grass seeds under some protecting hay. What meaning, I ask, walking out into this twittering world. There's a lesson here I could draw from the sunless sky and take with me into the tapering dark: on radiant mornings there's rarely a sound.

I was looking at the limbs of the knobby apple trees in the fog. Sparrows pecking. The mouse must have lost its head to cat or hawk. I haven't seen a scythe or power blade at work recently in the grass. I'd rather not be sucked into the gray tunnel of the morning.

I pulled into the dusty parking lot the next afternoon and rolled down the window to listen to the isolate clear cello sounds. Now there was someone practicing the piano up there, precise yet fluid.

When we got back to the cottage I followed my son into the yard, where he climbed toward the fork of the apple tree and said, "When you're a little boy again you can climb trees too."

I was looking out the window screen watching the world reappear. Reticulate shadow of the apple tree. The chopped-up distances of sea and sky looked like the mind's ruins, outcrop stone, settlement, thickets, vast sheets of blue broken by a boat. Two boys playing pirates on the rocks.

I was staring at the new telephone pole bisecting sea and sky when I remembered the abandoned quarry in Oceanville, the outsize clumps of pink granite, the osprey's nest on the telephone pole, the osprey's flight.

And when I returned again to the dusty lot the window on the second story of the church was half open and—not a sound.

I lay awake looking out the window screen into the dark trying to remember where I was when I found myself on the 35th floor of the Empire Hotel, walking reluctantly, with a drink in my hand, onto the terrace, trying to act normally while my stomach sank and my knees buckled and I was drawn to the rail.

I was staring out the window screen when the moon's eclipse began. Now the earth made the moon more visible, more isolate, more abstract. Orange at the edges, surrounded by char, like the fire I stare into this cold morning.

Post eclipse. I stared out the window screen. Shadows lengthened, logs burned down. An orange flame licked the edges. During the eclipse, when the earth's shadow was full on the full moon, you could see the moon as it really was and not as a light reflecting object. The moon which had always been a surface had become a depth.

I was looking out the window. This summer there's a new screen in it, bordered by a white frame. Sometimes I wish we had the old half-screen, the one we had to jam into the window frame.

I was looking out the window screen. A smoking hole appeared, like a shutter stopped down. I was looking at this dream:

We were on the border of Maryland and Virginia. We were in Maryland, but invited to a woman's house in Virginia, a gracious lady who received few visitors. I parted your knees as you slept and then you opened your eyes. We had a choice, to stay in Maryland for those two hours alone together or cross the border into Virginia and appear at the woman's house for tea. I parted your knees. You said you wouldn't say no, but that it would be bloody. And we only had half an hour before I had to leave to get the boy. When you opened your eyes you said you were dreaming of a lens zooming in and out.

THE PASSAGEWAY

That's his head up there on the screen.
Gazing at the cornucopia of bones,
the jaw's certitude in exposure,
he glimpses the narrowing passageway
between the fifth and sixth cervical vertebrae,
the glitch in the ganglia—

or it could be a bone spur
pressing into the soft tissue:
and the causes variable too,
an unremembered trauma—
the damage a metaphor
for what he'd done to his body in his life,
the far-ranging, incalculable abuse,
from birth-trauma to drugs, bad posture,
jogging, writing, *thinking,*
general recklessness—.

To his right two doctors are scanning
a uterus on another screen—
like a white-on-black sketch
of a mound or a mountain,
rising from a broad base,
narrowing, receding
by cliffs and scree:
some fibers there, no doubt,
"but not necessarily fibroids";
the diagnosis still in doubt,
the doctors staring intently
at the screen—. . . .

Does the uterus belong to the woman
signing in with him at radiology,

the tall woman with the rust-
colored hair who, he noticed,
glancing at her information sheet,
was born the same year as he—
(and she didn't look any older)
though she had "a serious problem. . . ."

For a moment in the waiting room,
with her hair falling to her shoulders as she shook her head,
he thought she might be another tall woman,
someone he knew in college, blond,
almost Amazonian: he'd looked up to her
for two years, never getting closer
than the spiralling, speech-impacting
turmoil of his own desire—
except one night,

an end to his longing
in sight, her long body
twisting and thrashing
like a net on his high bed
as he slid off her boots,
jeans, and lifted off her glasses,
when, all at once, they were eye to eye,
reflected in each other's pupils,
and as he slowly unbuttoned her silk shirt
she lay utterly still.

MY QUARREL WITH THOREAU

I went away to the woods to live all year
with no friends near, and when I read
Walden most of all I admired
your capacity for solitude.

And loathed my own weakness.
All autumn I wrote long letters to friends
about the hunter who wore a dusk-colored mask to trick deer;
the pheasant trapped inside the tennis court; mud.

No one took the bait; nature
was out of fashion that year.
In my father's hat, I turned
the wide brim down all the way around

and went for long walks alone in rainy November woods,
guided by stone fences
through cathedral forests where I waited
for the light to break.

Vision is what I sought.
You didn't go "into solitude."
Solitude is having no one to repair to.
You went home to mama every day.

Or for an early dinner cooked for you
by the Emersons or the Alcotts.
After setting fire to the woods
cooking trout in a tree stump

you took a room
at Walden Pond and made sure
everyone in town knew it.
One thing we had in common:

neither of us paid rent that year—
though I paid the price for house-sitting.
The retired Colonel who breezed in from Aruba
to find the top on the garbage can ajar,

was not so broad-minded as your landlord,
Mr. Emerson, but whenever my will
weakened and I longed for company
I reminded myself of how sensibly you broke

your day: reading, writing, hoeing.
And, still trusting in your words, that sincere
account of one's life you call for in a writer,
I thought of you in that hour

when I felt myself coming apart,
and, staring at my hands, I was reduced
to a pair of ears listening
for the crunch of tires on the gravel. . . .

But you lied in your sacred book.
I lied too, for I was not alone
but with a woman
(though she was gone from morning till night).

I too had in my own way set fire to the woods;
only it was in the mountains, and in the desert,
and by the sea where there were no trees or
grass to catch fire.

MOUND BUILDING:
(On the train, New York to Washington)

Tunnels: who can think of them
        as having variety,
unless we take the lines running through
        the dark holes

as openings for waste acreage,
        white boxcars
smeared with fog and posters,
        and under these mounds,

under these abandoned factories
        and colonnades
railroad ties turn up in a heap
        on a narrow rise

running through the outskirts,
        which is all there is,
some town center distinctly
        off center and then

the sky, like an outcast,
        drags a cape over the barrens
and the sign for the "Quaker Waxed
        Paper Co." disappears.

What is so harrowing
        about the innocent
pale sun's resemblance
        to the full moon

such as the one I will see
        tonight, rounding,
bringing me
        back, full circle,

120

to my son's mound building
        in his crib,
the way he roots around
        with his eyes clamped shut

bulldozing pillows and blankets
        and towels and toys
up against the rear,
        snorting and chuffling as if

crawling through ooze and then,
        climbing and crawling
to the peak where he
        falls asleep

like a mammoth in mid-strife
        caught in ice
or a fullback hurling himself
        over the pack,

the ball wedged against his armpit,
        time out until
the bars of the crib are no longer
        visible to him.

Not to obscure what I see
        in this half-light
with melancholy
        like an old painting

in an antique shop
        before it's been restored
and the varnish
        of centuries removed.

After so many scaffolds and frames
        piled on landscapes
under construction,
        (as if a horizontal

parenthesis were
        the sky's vault)
one longs for a river,
        one longs,

and it doesn't have to be
        as lovely as
the mouth of the Susquehanna,
        and for the light

to shine on the river,
        and for the river—
love of the world
        being all we have.

COURBET

1

Peasant life, Jura mountains, revolution.
Success, ruin.

Courbet's three sisters among the rocks of the field: pied clouds.
Thistles even now exploding from the foreground.

Foam at the edge of the cave's mouth, rippling over stones,
a man poling a raft toward the dark core,

undaunted, vertical as a post.
Terror of the horizontal, a human terror.

Let's look at this from the truer, inhuman point of view:
rocks and fields and lakes, splayed raggedly,

not a square or a circle, not even a round hole,
they torment the mind, these surfaces, being so close. . . .

Nature, in its casual perfection, offers no respite,
no matter how far we stray by day from the village bell

its tintinnabulation echoes and reverberates,
seeks out the wanderer in the woods,

plucks him from thickets and groves of beech trees
where the tinkling of cowbells, flat and toneless

in the mountain air, and the pastoral
music of a sunken time from parish churches

set him to dreaming about the tavern:
night and wine.

2

The Stonebreakers—destroyed when Dresden was bombed.
Photograph of a photograph, close-up of a close-up:

Courbet and labor: Chink of the pick.
The men with their backs to us.

The old man, on his knees,
crouched by the roadside

in the dust and summer heat,
straw hat, patched trousers, striped vest,

and through the chinks in his cracked shoes
faded blue socks revealing his heels.

The young man standing beside him as if the two
were one person at different stages of life.

Looked at like this, the universe is a cramped place.
What is will remain   unforgiven.

And in *The Winnowers* the woman
on her knees with her back to us,

sifting the wheat through the basket,
looks as if she's about to pray.

This is not what the two women
in *Young Women on the Banks of the Seine*

are doing, facing us with closed eyes,
forcing our eyes to meet theirs in reverie,

the women daydreaming the spectators
dreaming the women. . . .

3 *The Artist's Studio*

Courbet, brush in hand, at his easel, more at *ease*
than we will ever seen him again, reaching out
to dab some more black-green into the "trees,"

some gray-black into the "rocks,"
flanked by the naked model, the "muse,"
buxom, motherly, alluring, within sight, possibly within reach,

her nipples in line with his fingertips,
and the curious urchin, whose eyes we don't see. . . ;
the fair-haired rustic who looks as if he had stepped out

of the canvas to stare back at the painter's hand;
the child whose response we are not given,
(possibly the artist as a child, possibly the artist's child),

whose innocence and wonder we must draw from the angle
of his head gazing at whatever "detail" Courbet is about to lay
       onto the canvas,
as if the source of original light were the source of the Loue

whose waters rush through his arm as he holds fast
to the pulse and throb of the first impulse.
The Origin of the World.

4

The "real" Gustave Courbet. . . :

Courbet the wanderer, dressed in white, his beard aimed
at his patron Bruyas' chin, on the road to Sête near Montpellier.

"To be in a position to interpret the customs, the ideas, the
various aspects of the age as I see them, to be not only a
painter, but also a man, to make living art, that is my aim."

To apply the same eye to fops and laborers.
Equality   a dangerous truth.

To capture the avid surface.

Courbet and seeing:

The paint, laid down with a palette knife, crusting,
the eye stilled, arrested,
banishing illusion,
sending the dream into exile, no longer
to dream any dream but the dream of the real—

"There is only one other," he said, "who understands the sky."

5

Courbet and the unpeopled landscape and seascape:
the earth as it is without us.

Boats and masts on the shore, broken horizons, thickness
of waves, graininess of sand, the rocks   breakdown of particles.

Courbet broken, not enough sinew in the trees, snow
too white, the crows   not black enough.

Uneven ground the snow reveals, the snow conceals,
and above it all, blue shadows.

6

Alone now, in a prison courtyard in Sainte-Pélagie,
he stands at his ease, in his earth-

colored beret, smoking his pipe,
his foulard red as a torch geranium,

and finds three scrawny trees
beyond the unlatched window and the bars

searching for a glimmer of sunlight.
There are men who are consumed by the pressure

of seeing, all their senses directed to one end.
And something inhuman about them.

7

So many matters left untended:
Courbet and Fourier, Courbet and Jean Journet. . . .
The judgment day sky
in *The Valley of the Loue*
and the *Burial at Ornan,*

a sky that sucks its charcoal
out of caves and wells,
and tiers of white rocks flocking diagonally
across the gray sky,
and the other darkness, unseen but still

present, of night, waiting
for gravediggers to fill up that hole;
a night that is not night
but comes disguised as water as
it ripples over rocks or gathers

in bold storm clouds over the valley.
And a light, a light that is the light
of the Jura flooding Courbet's studio
in far away Paris.
Light that breaks off his raised

knife. And though we find ourselves
in open air the road is not open:
No one walks unburdened down these narrow lanes.
No one strolls.
Something stands in the way.

And the rocks' expressions, they are almost
thoughtful, as if from long gazing.
And the sky. What has happened to the sky?
Let's pass over the lists
of his imperfections,

remnants strewn over his decline
by those who would malign him
for not being who he wasn't;
for too much laughter,
for guzzling beer

with the air of a jeering peasant;
for not knowing more than the earth he knew,
the deep green valleys,
waters, and rocks of the Jura
where it is still possible to go.

CONVERSATION: DECEMBER, THE NIGHT CITY

Coffee and buffalo wings at Houlihan's.
Four luminous globes pass by on Broadway,
against gravity, against the grave,
and only when they had strayed
far into the sluggish rhythms
of the traffic did we see the bicycles' spokes
and the four figures in black, back to back.
She said, "You think I'm the Rock of Gibraltar
but I'm just a piece of sandstone
chipping away in the rain."

———

This light, this street, this sense
of possibility without limit—
our bodies will never know eternity
but we will know eternity
through our bodies;
the ache in my neck, the tingling
down your arm—
these impose limits.
And yet you say the place is wrong.

———

Steamshovels pour more tar into a hole—
a round hole and a hole
with the odd length and odd imprint
of a body fallen to earth—. . . .
The driver of the tarpaulined Mack cranes his head—
what's taking so long, he wonders,
why can't they get it done?

Night falls through soundless space.
Streetlights flicker
and cars fan their way
through the ambiguous light.

Nothing happens the same way twice.
And yet we court repetition.
And the milky sky above the city blurs
what lies above this sky.

Today the snow is falling
soundlessly, weightlessly,
in the ruins of New York.

———————

The eve of his fortieth birthday
he feels heavy-lidded at one
turns off the light and spends the hours till dawn

in anticipation.
Eros and the common good
flicker in his left eyelid

and his right.
Dawn sleep brings a dream of travelling
somewhere he has never been;

he wakes, exhausted
but not entirely
without hope.

———————

It was a time of conversations.
He was an older man, nearly twice my age,
who circled and circled a point.

130

I thought it would never arrive.
There was a film he happened to catch
on the CUNY cable station, early Bergman, *Winter Light,*
a minister in a small town, and a woman,
that summed up for him   a sense   of human
longing   and   unfulfillment
—just when I was about to interrupt
he came to his conclusion with an abrupt
twirl of his fingers.

————

The moon rose, bold and furious that night—
The moon, she says, as we cross the Square,
is the source of confusion: it's why
so many people are jumping out of windows
this week, look, it swells like a melon,
looks like it could topple out of the black sky,
but we're in the wrong lunar phase—

what you think you see is two days away.

————

And though I dream this night of the desert
when I wake my first thought is—
there is also the present, there was, yesterday,
the eternal ride over the rumbling bridge,
the lights of the city still mysterious—if scrutable—
the dark pouring of the East River. . . .

Vast spray of buildings.

Every kind of light but starlight.

BIOGRAPHICAL NOTE

Mark Rudman was born in New York City, and grew up in the Midwest and West. His *By Contraries: Poems 1970–84* appeared in 1987. His other books include *Robert Lowell: An Introduction to the Poetry*, and a translation of Bohdan Boychuk's selected poems, *Memories of Love*, done in collaboration with the author. He has received the Academy of American Poets Prize, the Max Hayward Award for his translation of Boris Pasternak's *My Sister—Life*, fellowships in poetry from the Yaddo, Ingram Merrill Foundation and the New York Foundation of the Arts, and in translation of poetry from the P.E.N. Translation Center. His poems have appeared in a wide number of magazines and anthologies including *The Atlantic Monthly*, *Harper's*, *Ironwood*, *The New Republic*, *The New Yorker*, *The New Directions Annual*, *The Paris Review*, and *The Best American Poetry 1989*. He is presently completing a translation of *The Trojan Woman* for the Oxford Series of Greek Tragedies and *Diverse Voices*, a book of essays on poetry and poetics. He lives in New York City with his wife and son. He teaches in the writing programs at Columbia University and New York University and is editor of the literary magazine *Pequod*.